Holy Week Prayer Book

Palm Sunday through Holy Saturday

for the

Community of the Gospel

BeneVentura, LLC
PO Box 414
Hortonville, WI 54944

D0887088

First Edition, April 2015

Printed in the United States of America

ISBN 978-0-692-39992-7

Holy Week
Prayer Book

Palm Sunday through Holy Saturday

Other related books...

Reclaiming Eden

Reclaiming Your Soul

Christmas Season Prayer Book

Nothing can separate us from the love of God; even when we fail to recognize Him in ourselves or others - even though the depth of mankind's separation from God led to the death of Jesus Christ on the cross - God will find a way to bring each one of us back to Him, to complete our journey.

Introduction

The Community of the Gospel was formed as a response to the Great Commandments: "You shall love the Lord your God with all your heart, and with all your soul, and with all your mind." And, "You shall love your neighbor as yourself."

We are a non-residential Monastic Community whose members try to help each other on their spiritual journeys. We do this by living a monastic life of daily prayer, reflective study, and personal service while remaining in the secular world. We seek to demonstrate our faith in unique ways as best we can, while allowing our lives to be transformed by God.

Our Community is...

Gospel-centered - The core of our being comes from the teaching and grace of the Living Word. We hope to be examples of the Gospel message. Our strength and healing power comes from the knowledge of the Gospel - we are a group of like-minded people seeking the love of Christ that transcends our shortcomings and those of the world around us. We continue to grow and learn together, finding the way to His Truth.

Ecumenical - Although based in the Episcopal Church, we welcome any Christian seeker who shares our values and desires to fully know, love, and serve the Lord.

Faith-based - We know that we are saved through faith, but we demonstrate our faith through actively practicing monastic principles of prayer, study and service in unique ways.

i

Inclusive - acceptance into the Community is based on one's desire to share in the treasures of love and compassion of Our Lord. It is not based on age, gender, marital status, sexual orientation, academic achievement or ethnicity.

Non-residential - Our members live and work in various places, but are connected by the love and wisdom of Christ. Our spiritual home is in the heart of Christ.

Contemplative and Action-oriented - we strive to blend the contemplative life with a life of action in a spirit of collaboration. The contemplative life gives us the strength, wisdom and desire to use our talents and abilities in the world, and the world of action provides us with material for further prayer and contemplation.

Although we are primarily a dispersed community (we live and work in various parts of the world), we travel together as one in spirit with Our Lord. We believe that our purpose is to awaken to God's wisdom and love, and to shape our lives following God's principles. The expression of our personal mission in life is a response to the love of God who made each of us in a unique way. We join together as the body of Christ to share our journey and our resources as we are able, and to mutually encourage each other's faith journey.

The Charism of this Community is to live the monastic vows of Daily Prayer, Reflective Study and Personal Service that lead to nurturing of the soul at the hands and heart of Christ. This results in our knowing, loving and serving the Lord in our own unique way, as God made us.

Members become transformed by living what we value. Not that these things in themselves do the transforming, but they put us in a position whereby we can be transformed by the love of God.

Our Core Vows…

For thousands of years people have been striving to open the pathways of life to receive the enduring love of God. Frequently, these pathways rest in devotion, knowledge, and action. The vows we hold dearest reflect these three ancient, sacred pathways. They are the foundation of our monastic practice; this is what we do and who we are.

Prayer is how we express the Way of Devotion. We view this vow to mean spending time daily in the presence of God during prayer and meditation. Our Members will usually pray 1 to 4 times daily, using a format that suits their individual prayer temperament. Our prayer time is "spiritual breathing." It is a time when we take in His love and compassion for us and for the world, and then share this with others through thanksgiving, praise, intercessions and supplications.

While we have several Community Prayer Books, members are encouraged to explore Prayer Books in a variety of formats. This particular Prayer Book guides the participant through Morning and Evening Prayer from Palm Sunday through Holy Saturday. (It's assumed that corporate worship would be used for the Sunday services.) The next page provides some suggestions for using this Prayer Book.

Blessings to you on your journey!

Concerning the Holy Week Office

The Good Friday Office portion of this Prayer Book can be offered at one sitting, or it can be followed according to the times suggested. By using the times, the participant may get a better sense for the actual events of that day.

Prayer time is like a good meal, so don't rush through it. Say them slowly and savor them. Leave silence (30 seconds or so) between parts or where silence is indicated.

It is suggested that you offer your prayers following a 15-20 minute Centering Prayer/Presence. This will help prepare your mind and spirit for the service.

Sunday Mass takes precedence over Morning Prayer.

Some readings from the Gospel are compilations of multiple Gospels as their scripture provides.

The rubrics for standing and sitting are optional, and depend on whether the prayer is being offered by an individual or a small group.

When candles are used, whenever possible, they should be lit by a female, signifying that the Blessed Virgin Mary brought the Light into the world.

Additional Collects and prayers may be added as desired.

Neck crosses, prayer shawls and stoles may be worn at any time by anyone offering the prayers.

Noonday prayer and Compline may be offered using another suitable format.

Palm Sunday
The Entrance

EVENING PRAYER

I. Invitatory

The officiant opens with this sentence: (All stand)

"Hosanna to the Son of David! Blessed is he who comes in the name of the Lord! Hosanna in the highest!"
(Matthew 21:9)

O God, make speed to save us.
O Lord, make haste to help us.

Glory to the Father, and to the Son,
and to the Holy Spirit. *
**As it was in the beginning, is now,
and will be for ever. Amen.**

Phos Hilaron

O gracious Light, pure brightness of the ever-living Father in heaven, *
O Jesus Christ, holy and blessed!

Now as we have come to the setting of the sun, and our eyes behold the vesper light, *
We sing your praises, O God: Father, Son and Holy Spirit.

You are worthy at all times to be praised by happy voices, O Son of God, O Giver of life, *
And to be glorified through all the worlds.

1

Psalm

The Lord is God, and He has given us the Light;
Bind the festal procession with branches!

Psalm 118:19-26

Open to me the gates of holiness, *
    I will enter and give thanks.
This is the Lord's own gate, *
    where the awakened may enter.
I will thank you for you have answered *
    and you are my Savior.
The stone which the builders rejected *
    has become the corner stone.
This is the work of the Lord, *
    a marvel in our eyes.
This is a day the Lord has made; *
    Let us rejoice and be glad.
O Lord, grant us salvation; *
    O Lord, grant us deliverance.
Blessed in the name of the Lord *
    is he who comes.
We bless you from the house of the Lord, *
    the Lord God is our Light.
Go forward in procession with branches *
    even to the altar.
You are my God, I thank you. *
    My God, I praise you.
Give thanks to the Lord who is good; *
    For God's love endures forever.

Glory to the Father, and to the Son,
and to the Holy Spirit. *
**As it was in the beginning, is now,
and will be for ever. Amen.**

The Lord is God, and He has given us the Light;
Bind the festal procession with branches!

II. The Lessons   *(Be seated)*

Old Testament Lesson

A reading from the Book of Zechariah (9:9-10)

Rejoice greatly, O daughter Zion!
    Shout aloud, O daughter Jerusalem!
Lo, your king comes to you;
    triumphant and victorious is he,
humble and riding on a donkey,
    on a colt, the foal of a donkey.
He will cut off the chariot from Ephraim
    and the warhorse from Jerusalem;
and the battle-bow shall be cut off,
    and he shall command peace to the nations;
his dominion shall be from sea to sea,
    and from the River to the ends of the earth.

The Word of the Lord.

Silence for reflection.

Canticle (The Prologue of John)

In the beginning was the Word,
　　And the Word was with God.
And the Word was God,
　　He was in the beginning with God.
All things were made through him,
　　And without him was not anything made
that was made.
In him was life,
　　And the life was the light of the human race.
The light shines in the darkness,
　　And the darkness has never overcome it.
He was in the world, and the world was made
through him,
　　Yet the world knew him not.
He came to his own home,
　　And his own people would not receive him.
But to all who received him, who believed on his name,
　　He has given power to become children of God.
They were born not of blood, nor of the will of the flesh,
　　Nor of any human will, but of God.
And the Word became flesh,
　　And dwelt among us, full of grace and truth.
We have seen his glory,
　　Glory as of the only Son from the Father.
And from his fullness we have all received,
　　Even grace upon grace.

Reading of the Gospel *(All stand)*

The Holy Gospel of Our Lord Jesus Christ:

When they were approaching Jerusalem, at
Bethphage and Bethany, near the Mount of Olives, he sent
two of his disciples and said to them, "Go into the village
ahead of you, and immediately as you enter it, you will find
a donkey tied, and a colt with her that has never been
ridden; untie them and bring them to me. If anyone says to
you, 'Why are you doing this?' just say this, 'The Lord
needs it and will send it back here immediately.'" This took
place to fulfill what had been spoken through the prophet,
saying, 'Tell the daughter of Zion, Look, your king is
coming to you, humble, and mounted on a donkey, and on a
colt, the foal of a donkey.'
They went away and found a colt tied near a door,
outside in the street. As they were untying it, some of the
bystanders said to them, "What are you doing, untying the
colt?" They told them what Jesus had said; and they allowed
them to take it. Then they brought the colt to Jesus and after
they threw their cloaks on it; they sat Jesus on it. The crowd
that had been with him when he called Lazarus out of the
tomb and raised him from the dead continued to testify. It
was also because they heard that he had performed this sign
that the crowd went to meet him. They spread their cloaks
on the road, and others took branches of palm trees.
As he was now approaching the path down from the
Mount of Olives, the whole multitude of the disciples began
to praise God joyfully with a loud voice for all the deeds of
power that they had seen, saying, "Hosanna to the Son of
David! Blessed is the one who comes in the name of the
Lord! Blessed is the coming kingdom of our ancestor
David! Hosanna in the highest heaven!" When he entered
Jerusalem, the whole city was in turmoil, asking, "Who is
this?" The crowds were saying, "This is the prophet Jesus
from Nazareth in Galilee."

Some of the Pharisees in the crowd said to him, "Teacher, order your disciples to stop." He answered, "I tell you, if these were silent, the stones would shout out." The Pharisees then said to one another, "You see, you can do nothing. Look, the world has gone after him!"

As he came near and saw the city, he wept over it, saying, "If you, even you, had only recognized on this day the things that make for peace! But now they are hidden from your eyes. Indeed, the days will come upon you, when your enemies will set up ramparts around you and surround you, and hem you in on every side. They will crush you to the ground, you and your children within you, and they will not leave within you one stone upon another; because you did not recognize the time of your visitation from God." His disciples did not understand these things at first; but when Jesus was glorified, then they remembered that these things had been written of him and had been done to him.

Then he entered Jerusalem and stopped at the temple; and when he had looked around at everything, as it was already late, he went out to Bethany with the twelve.

The Gospel of the Lord.

Praise be to You, O Christ. *(Be seated)*

Silence for reflection, homily or reading.
[How would you describe Christ's entrance into your life? Are you willing to lay down your "outer cloak" to let him in?]

Magnificat

My soul proclaims the greatness of the Lord*
    My spirit rejoices in God my Savior.
You have looked with favor on your humble servant*
    And all generations will call me blessed.
You, O God, have done great things for me*
    And holy is your name.
You have mercy on those who love you*
    From generation to generation.
You have shown the strength of your arm*
    And have scattered the proud in their conceit.
You have cast down the mighty from their thrones*
    And have lifted up the lowly,
You have filled the hungry with good things*
    And the rich you have sent away empty.
You have come to the help of your people*
    For you remembered your promise of mercy.
The promise you made to our forbears*
    To Abraham and his children forever.

Lord, O Blessed Love.
Christ, O Blessed Light.
Lord, O Blessed Love.

Rejoice! Rejoice!
Emmanuel shall come to you, O Israel.

III. The Prayers

The Lord be with you.
And also with you.

The Lord's Prayer   *(Stand facing altar)*

Our Father in heaven, hallowed be your name,
    Your kingdom come, your will be done,
    On earth as it is in heaven.
Give us today our daily bread. Forgive us, as we forgive
others.
    Save us from the time of trial,
 and deliver us from evil.
For the kingdom, the power, and the glory are yours
    Now and forever. Amen

Additional Prayers may be added here.

Collect

Almighty and ever-living God, in your tender love toward
us you sent your Son to take our nature upon him, to live
with us and to teach us and to heal us; grant that we may
follow the example of his great humility and share in his
glorious life and resurrection; who lives and reigns with you
and the Holy Spirit, one God, now and forever. Amen.

May the Risen Christ convince you that God loves you and
guides you. **Amen.**

Let us bless the Lord.
Thanks be to God.

Holy Monday
Cleansing of the Temple

MORNING PRAYER

I. Invitatory

The officiant opens with this sentence (All stand)

Do you not know that you are God's temple and that God's Spirit dwells in you? (I Corinthians 3:16)

All the ends of the earth *
Shall see the salvation of our God.
Isaiah 52

O Lord, Open our lips. *
And our mouth shall proclaim Your praise.

Glory to the Father, and to the Son,
and to the Holy Spirit. *
As it was in the beginning, is now,
and will be for ever. Amen.

Psalm

In the beginning was the Word, *
And the Word was with God, and the Word was God.

from Psalm 51

Have mercy on me, O God, *
    According to your steadfast love.
According to your abundant mercy *
    Blot out my offenses.
You desire truth in the inward being, *
    Therefore teach me wisdom in my heart.
Purge me with hyssop, and I shall be clean, *
    Wash me, and I shall be cleaner than snow.
Create in me a clean heart, O God, *
    And renew a right spirit within me.
Cast me not away from your presence, *
    And take not your Holy Spirit from me.
O Lord, open my lips, *
    And my mouth shall show your praise.
You have no delight in sacrifice, *
    Unless it is a contrite heart.

Glory to the Father, and to the Son,
and to the Holy Spirit. *
As it was in the beginning, is now,
and will be for ever. Amen.

In the beginning was the Word, *
And the Word was with God, and the Word was God.

II. The Lessons   *(Be seated)*

Old Testament Lesson

A reading from the book of Isaiah (56:6-8)

And the foreigners who join themselves to the Lord, to
minister to him, to love the name of the Lord, and to be his
servants, all who keep the Sabbath, and do not profane it,
and hold fast my covenant – these I will bring to my holy
mountain, and make them joyful in my house of prayer;
their burnt offerings and their sacrifices will be accepted on
my altar; for my house shall be called a house of prayer for
all peoples. Thus says the Lord God, who gathers the
outcasts of Israel, I will gather others to them besides those
already gathered.

The word of the Lord.

Silence for reflection.

Canticle

Jesus, Savior, pilot me
Over life's tempestuous sea;
Unknown waves before me roll,
Hiding rock and treacherous shoal;
Chart and compass come from Thee;
Jesus, Savior, pilot me.

As a mother stills her child,
Thou canst hush the ocean wild;
Boisterous waves obey Thy will
When Thou say to them, "Be still."
Wondrous Sovereign of the sea,
Jesus, Savior, pilot me.

When at last I near the shore,
And the fearful breakers roar;
'Twixt me and the peaceful rest,
Then, while leaning on Thy breast,
May I hear Thee say to me,
"Fear not, I will pilot thee."

Edward Hopper, 1871

Reading of the Gospel *(All stand)*

The Holy Gospel of Our Lord Jesus Christ:

In the morning, returning to the city, he was hungry.
And seeing a fig tree by the side of the road, he went to it
and found nothing at all on it but leaves. Then he said to it,
"May no fruit ever come from you again!" And the fig tree
withered at once. When the disciples saw it, they were
amazed, saying, "How did the fig tree wither at once?"
Jesus answered them, "Truly I tell you, if you have faith and
do not doubt, not only will you do what has been done to
the fig tree, but even if you say to this mountain, 'Be lifted
up and thrown into the sea', it will be done. Whatever you
ask for in prayer with faith, you will receive."
Then they came to Jerusalem. And he entered the temple
and began to drive out those who were selling and those
who were buying in the temple, and he overturned the tables
of the money-changers and the seats of those who sold
doves; and he would not allow anyone to carry anything
through the temple. He was teaching and saying, "Is it not
written, 'My house shall be called a house of prayer for all
the nations'? But you have made it a den of robbers."

The word of the Lord. *Be seated.*

Silence for reflection, homily or reading.

[The fig tree may represent the established system that no
longer feeds people's hearts. Since it doesn't feed people
properly, it would no longer bear fruit. Jesus continued this
message by cleaning out the temple – removing things that
are contrary to his message of love and compassion. What
might need to be cleaned out of your 'temple'?]

13

Benedictus

Blessed are you O Lord our God*
You have come to your people and set them free.
You have raised up for us a mighty Savior*
Born of the house of your servant David.
Through your holy prophets you promised of old*
That you would save us from our enemies,
From the hands of all who hate us.
You promised to show mercy to our forbears*
And to remember your holy covenant.
This was the oath you swore to our father Abraham*
To set us free from the hands of our enemies,
Free to worship you without fear*
Holy and righteous in your sight all the days of our life.
And you, child, shall be called the prophet of the Most High*
For you will go before the Lord to prepare the way,
To give God's people knowledge of salvation*
Through the forgiveness of their sins.
In the tender compassion of our God*
The dawn from on high shall break upon us.
To shine on those who dwell in darkness and the shadow of death*
And to guide our feet into the way of peace.

Glory to the Father, and to the Son,
and to the Holy Spirit. *
**As it was in the beginning, is now,
and will be for ever. Amen.**

III. The Prayers

The Lord be with you all.
And also with you.

The Lord's Prayer   *(Stand facing altar)*

Our Father in heaven, hallowed be your name,
    Your kingdom come, your will be done,
    On earth as it is in heaven.
Give us today our daily bread. Forgive us, as we forgive
others.
    Save us from the time of trial,
and deliver us from evil.
For the kingdom, the power, and the glory are yours
    Now and forever. Amen

Additional Prayers may be added here.

Collect

Teach us, O Spirit, how to live and worship, without being
worldly or greedy. Drive from our lives what spoils them,
and make us temples of Your love through Jesus Christ,
who lives and reigns with You and the Holy Spirit, one
God, in glory everlasting. Amen.

The grace of Our Lord Jesus Christ, and the love of God,
and the companionship of the Holy Spirit, be in us and
those absent from us. **Amen.**

Let us bless the Lord. **Thanks be to God.**

EVENING PRAYER

I. Invitatory

The officiant opens with this sentence: (All stand)

Set your minds on things that are above,
and not on things that are of mankind's.

O God, make speed to save us.
O Lord, make haste to help us.

Glory to the Father, and to the Son,
and to the Holy Spirit. *
**As it was in the beginning, is now,
and will be for ever. Amen.**

Phos Hilaron

O gracious Light, pure brightness
of the ever-living Father in heaven, *
O Jesus Christ, holy and blessed!

Now as we have come to the setting of the sun, and our eyes
behold the vesper light, *
**We sing your praises, O God: Father, Son and Holy
Spirit.**

You are worthy at all times to be praised by happy voices,
O Son of God, O Giver of life, *
And to be glorified through all the worlds.

Psalm *(Be seated)*

This is the day the Lord has made; *
Let us rejoice and be glad in it.

from Psalm 36

Your steadfast love, O Lord, extends to the heavens. *
   Your faithfulness to the clouds.
Your righteousness is like the mighty mountains, *
   Your judgments are like the great deep.
You save humans and animals alike, O Lord. *
   How precious is your steadfast love!
All people may take refuge, *
   In the shadow of your wings.
They feast on the abundance of your house, *
   And they drink from the river of your delights.
For the fountain of life is with you, *
   In your Light we see Light.
Continue your love to all peoples, *
   And your salvation to the upright of heart.

Glory to the Father, and to the Son,
and to the Holy Spirit. *
**As it was in the beginning, is now,
and will be for ever. Amen.**

This is the day the Lord has made; *
Let us rejoice and be glad in it.

II. The Lessons

Old Testament Lesson

A reading from the book of Jeremiah (17)

Blessed are those who trust in the Lord, whose trust is the Lord. They shall be like a tree planted by water, sending out its roots by the stream. It shall not fear when heat comes, and its leaves shall stay green. I the Lord test the mind and search the heart, to give to all according to their ways. Heal me, O Lord, and I shall be healed; save me, and I shall be saved; for you are my praise.

The Word of the Lord.

Silence for reflection. Be seated.

Canticle

Hosanna to the living Lord!
Hosanna to the incarnate Word!
To Christ, Creator, Savior, King,
Let earth, let heaven, hosanna sing!

Hosanna Lord! Thine angels cry;
Hosanna Lord! Thy saints reply;
Above us, beneath us, and around,
Both dead and living swell the sound!

O Savior, with protecting care,
Eternal! Bid thy Spirit rest;
And make our sacred soul to be
A temple pure and worthy thee.

From Reginald Haber (1783-1826)

18

Reading of the Gospel *(All stand)*

The Holy Gospel of Our Lord Jesus Christ:

The blind and the lame came to him in the temple, and he cured them. But when the chief priests and the scribes saw the amazing things that he did, and heard the children crying out in the temple, 'Hosanna to the Son of David', they became angry and said to him, 'Do you hear what these are saying?' Jesus said to them, 'Yes; have you never read, "Out of the mouths of infants and nursing babies you have prepared praise for yourself"?

And when the chief priests and the scribes heard it, they kept looking for a way to kill him; for they were afraid of him, because the whole crowd was spellbound by his teaching. And when evening came, Jesus and his disciples went out of the city.

The Gospel of the Lord.
Praise be to You, O Christ.

Be seated. Silence for reflection, homily or reading.

[To some, the Light of Christ brings joy. To others, it brings fear and trembling. The world of prejudice, greed, power, and illusion melt away in the Light of his love. Can you see why Jesus was in danger?]

Magnificat

My soul proclaims the greatness of the Lord*

    My spirit rejoices in God my Savior.

You have looked with favor on your humble servant*

    And all generations will call me blessed.

You, O God, have done great things for me*

    And holy is your name.

You have mercy on those who love you*

    From generation to generation.

You have shown the strength of your arm*

    And have scattered the proud in their conceit.

You have cast down the mighty from their thrones*

    And have lifted up the lowly,

You have filled the hungry with good things*

    And the rich you have sent away empty.

You have come to the help of your people*

    For you remembered your promise of mercy.

The promise you made to our forbears*

    To Abraham and his children forever.

Lord, O Blessed Love.
Christ, O Blessed Light.
Lord, O Blessed Love.

III. The Prayers

The Lord be with you.
And also with you.

The Lord's Prayer   *(Stand facing altar)*

Our Father in heaven, hallowed be your name,
   Your kingdom come, your will be done,
   On earth as it is in heaven.
Give us today our daily bread. Forgive us, as we forgive
others.
   Save us from the time of trial,
and deliver us from evil.
For the kingdom, the power, and the glory are yours
   Now and forever. Amen

Additional Prayers may be added here.

Collect

Almighty God, for our sake Your Son became incarnate,
and showed us Your love for us, even when he was put on a
cross; purify our hearts and grant us zeal in Your service,
through Jesus Christ our Lord, who lives and reigns with
you, in the unity of the Holy Spirit, one God, now and
forever. **Amen.**

May Christ, whose love for us could not be destroyed even
by death on a cross, give you all courage and joy in
believing. **Amen.**

Let us bless the Lord.   **Thanks be to God.**

Holy Tuesday
Teaching in the Temple

MORNING PRAYER

I. Invitatory

The officiant opens with this sentence: (All stand)

God so loved the world that he sent his only begotten Son, that whosoever would believe in him would not perish, but have everlasting life. John 3:16

You came to be with us to set us free, *
By your wisdom we leave the darkness.

O Lord, Open our lips. *
And our mouth shall proclaim Your praise.

Glory to the Father, and to the Son,
and to the Holy Spirit. *
As it was in the beginning, is now,
and will be for ever. Amen.

Psalm   *from Psalm 78*

In love God sent his Son to save, *
Not to condemn mankind.

Give ear, O my people, to my teaching; *
incline your ears to the words of my mouth.
I will open my mouth in a parable; *
I will utter dark sayings from of old,
things that we have heard and known, *
that our ancestors have told us.
We will not hide them from their children; *
we will tell to the coming generation
the glorious deeds of the LORD, and his might, *
and the wonders that he has done.
He established a decree in Jacob, *
and appointed a law in Israel,
which he commanded our ancestors *
to teach to their children;
that the next generation might know them, *
the children yet unborn,
and rise up and tell them to their children, *
so that they should set their hope in God,
and that they should not be like their ancestors, *
a stubborn and rebellious generation,
a generation whose heart was not steadfast, *
whose spirit was not faithful to God.

Glory to the Father, and to the Son,
and to the Holy Spirit. *
**As it was in the beginning, is now,
and will be for ever. Amen.**

In love God sent his Son to save, *
Not to condemn mankind.

23

II. The Lessons *(Be seated)*

Old Testament Lesson

A reading from the book of Isaiah (51:4-8)

Listen to me, my people, and give heed to me, my nation; for a teaching will go out from me, and my justice for a light to the peoples. I will bring near my deliverance swiftly, my salvation has gone out and my arms will rule the peoples; the coastlands wait for me, and for my arm they hope. Lift up your eyes to the heavens, and look at the earth beneath; for the heavens will vanish like smoke, the earth will wear out like a garment, and those who live on it will die like gnats; but my salvation will be forever, and my deliverance will never be ended.

The word of the Lord.

Silence for reflection.

Canticle

The great Creator of the worlds,
The sovereign God of heaven,
His holy and immortal truth
To all on earth hath given.

He sent no angel of his host
To bear this mighty Word,
But through him whose love is most,
The everlasting Lord.

He sent him not in wrath and power,
But grace and peace to bring;
In kindness, as a king might send
his son, Himself a king.

He sent him down as sending God;
In flesh to us he came;
As one with us he dwelt with us,
And bore a human name.

He came as Savior to his own,
The way of love he trod;
He came to win us by good will,
For force is not of God.

Not to oppress, but to summon all,
Their truest life to find,
In love God sent his Son to save,
Not to condemn mankind.

From Epistle to Diognetus, ca. 150

Reading of the Gospel *(All stand)*

The Holy Gospel of Our Lord Jesus Christ according to Matthew (22:34-40)

When the Pharisees heard that he had silenced the Sadducees, they gathered together, and one of them, a lawyer, asked him a question to test him. "Teacher, which commandment in the law is the greatest?" He said to him, "You shall love the Lord your God with all your heart, and with all your soul, and with all your mind. This is the greatest and first commandment. And a second is like it: You shall love your neighbor as yourself. On these two commandments hang all the law and the prophets."

The Gospel of the Lord.
Praise be to You, O Christ.

Be seated. Silence for reflection, homily or reading.

[How can we know what the right path is? How can we discern the truth? These two commandments can serve as our chief guideposts. The key word within both is love.]

Benedictus

Blessed are you O Lord our God*
You have come to your people and set them free.
You have raised up for us a mighty Savior*
Born of the house of your servant David.
Through your holy prophets you promised of old*
That you would save us from our enemies,
From the hands of all who hate us.
You promised to show mercy to our forbears*
And to remember your holy covenant.
This was the oath you swore to our father Abraham*
To set us free from the hands of our enemies,
Free to worship you without fear*
Holy and righteous in your sight all the days of our life.
And you, child, shall be called the prophet of the Most High*
For you will go before the Lord to prepare the way,
To give God's people knowledge of salvation*
Through the forgiveness of their sins.
In the tender compassion of our God*
The dawn from on high shall break upon us.
To shine on those who dwell in darkness and the shadow of death*
And to guide our feet into the way of peace.

Glory to the Father, and to the Son,
and to the Holy Spirit. *
**As it was in the beginning, is now,
and will be for ever. Amen.**

III. The Prayers

The Lord be with you all.
And also with you.

The Lord's Prayer *(Stand facing altar)*

Our Father in heaven, hallowed be your name,
Your kingdom come, your will be done,
On earth as it is in heaven.
Give us today our daily bread. Forgive us, as we forgive others.
Save us from the time of trial,
and deliver us from evil.
For the kingdom, the power, and the glory are yours
Now and forever. Amen

Additional Prayers may be added here.

Collect

Almighty God, You have made known your love to us through Jesus's life and word; Help us to receive his teaching, to find the fullness of that love and bring its fragrance to others, through Jesus Christ our Lord, who lives and reigns with you and the Holy Spirit, one God, forever and ever, Amen.

The grace of Our Lord Jesus Christ, and the love of God, and the companionship of the Holy Spirit, be in us and those absent from us. **Amen.**

Let us bless the Lord. **Thanks be to God.**

EVENING PRAYER

I. Invitatory

The officiant opens with this sentence: (All stand)

We praise you, O Lord, for being our guide,
because your teachings fill our hearts.

O God, make speed to save us. *
O Lord, make haste to help us.

Glory to the Father, and to the Son,
and to the Holy Spirit. *
**As it was in the beginning, is now,
and will be for ever. Amen.**

Phos Hilaron

O gracious Light, pure brightness of the ever-living Father
in heaven, *
O Jesus Christ, holy and blessed!

Now as we have come to the setting of the sun, and our eyes
behold the vesper light, *
**We sing your praises, O God: Father, Son and Holy
Spirit.**

You are worthy at all times to be praised by happy voices,
O Son of God, O Giver of life, *
And to be glorified through all the worlds.

Psalm

Take from our souls the strain and stress, *
With the beauty of your peace.

Psalm 119 (1-8)

Happy are those whose way is blameless, *
  who walk in the law of the LORD.
Happy are those who keep his decrees, *
  who seek him with their whole heart,
who also do no wrong, *
  but walk in his ways.
You have commanded your precepts *
  to be kept diligently.
O that my ways may be steadfast *
  in keeping your statutes!
Then I shall not be put to shame, *
  having my eyes fixed on all your commandments.
I will praise you with an upright heart, *
  when I learn your righteous ordinances.
I will observe your statutes; *
  do not utterly forsake me.

Glory to the Father, and to the Son,
and to the Holy Spirit. *
**As it was in the beginning, is now,
and will be for ever. Amen.**

Take from our souls the strain and stress, *
With the beauty of your peace.

II. The Lessons   *(Be seated)*

Old Testament Lesson

A reading from the book of Isaiah (chapter 42)

Here is my servant, whom I uphold, my chosen, in whom my soul delights; I have put my Spirit upon him; he will bring forth justice to the nations. He will not yell or lift up his voice, or make it heard on the street; a bruised reed he will not break, and a dimly burning wick he will not quench; he will faithfully bring forth justice. He will not grow faint or be crushed until he has established justice on the earth; and the coastlands wait for his teaching. I have given you a covenant to the people, a Light to the nations, to open the eyes that are blind, to bring out the prisoners from the dungeon of darkness. Sing to the Lord a new song!

The Word of the Lord.

Silence for reflection.

Canticle

Dear Lord and Father of mankind,
Forgive our foolish ways!
Reclothe us in our rightful mind,
In deeper reverence, praise.

O Sabbath rest by Galilee!
O calm of hills above,
Where Jesus knelt to share with thee,
Interpreted by love!

Drop thy still dews of quietness,
Till all our strivings cease;
Take from our souls the strain and stress,
With the beauty of your peace.
.
Breathe through the heat of our desire
Thy coolness and thy balm;
Speak through the earthquake, wind and fire,
O still, small voice of calm.

Adapted from John Greenleaf Whittier (1807-1892)

Reading of the Gospel *(All stand)*

The Holy Gospel of Our Lord Jesus Christ according to
Matthew (21:28-32)

"What do you think? A man had two sons; he went to the
first and said, 'Son, go and work in the vineyard today.' He
answered, 'I will not'; but later he changed his mind and
went. The father went to the second and said the same; and
he answered, 'I go, sir'; but he did not go. Which of the two
did the will of his father?" They said, "The first." Jesus said
to them, "Truly I tell you, the tax-collectors and the
prostitutes are going into the kingdom of God ahead of you.
For John came to you in the way of righteousness and you
did not believe him, but the tax-collectors and the
prostitutes believed him; and even after you saw it, you did
not change your minds and believe him."

The Gospel of the Lord.
Praise be to You, O Christ.

Be seated. Silence for reflection, homily or reading.

[It is when our thoughts, words, and deeds are all in
alignment with God's love in our lives that we are truly on
his path. But they aren't always in alignment, are they? We
must rely on our Observer soul then to discern the correct
course with the help of the Holy Spirit to "change our mind
and go."]

Magnificat

My soul proclaims the greatness of the Lord*

　　My spirit rejoices in God my Savior.

You have looked with favor on your humble servant*

　　And all generations will call me blessed.

You, O God, have done great things for me*

　　And holy is your name.

You have mercy on those who love you*

　　From generation to generation.

You have shown the strength of your arm*

　　And have scattered the proud in their conceit.

You have cast down the mighty from their thrones*

　　And have lifted up the lowly,

You have filled the hungry with good things*

　　And the rich you have sent away empty.

You have come to the help of your people*

　　For you remembered your promise of mercy.

The promise you made to our forbears*

　　To Abraham and his children forever.

Lord, O Blessed Love.
Christ, O Blessed Light.
Lord, O Blessed Love.

III. The Prayers

The Lord be with you.
And also with you.

The Lord's Prayer *(Stand facing altar)*

Our Father in heaven, hallowed be your name,
Your kingdom come, your will be done,
On earth as it is in heaven.
Give us today our daily bread. Forgive us, as we forgive others.
Save us from the time of trial,
and deliver us from evil.
For the kingdom, the power, and the glory are yours
Now and forever. Amen

Additional Prayers may be added here.

Collect

Almighty God, by our baptism into the life and resurrection of your Son Jesus Christ, you turn us from the old life of darkness to a new life of Light; Grant that we, being reborn to this new life in him, may live in his love all our days, seeking justice, peace, and the dignity of all persons, through Jesus Christ our Lord, who lives and reigns with you and the Holy Spirit, one God, now and for ever. Amen.

Let us bless the Lord.   **Thanks be to God.**

Holy Wednesday
The Light versus Darkness

MORNING PRAYER

I. Invitatory

The officiant opens with this sentence: (All stand)

I have come into the world as a Light and no one who believes in me will stay in darkness. (John 12)

Come Emmanuel!
God with us!

O Lord, Open our lips. *
And our mouth shall proclaim Your praise.

Glory to the Father, and to the Son,
and to the Holy Spirit. *
**As it was in the beginning, is now,
and will be for ever. Amen.**

Psalm

Awaken my soul, awaken to Light, *
Send the darkness off in flight.

Psalm 74:18-23

Remember this, O LORD, how the enemy scoffs, *

and an impious people reviles your name.

Do not deliver the soul of your dove to the wild animals; *

do not forget the life of your poor for ever.

Have regard for your covenant, *

for the dark places of the land are full of the haunts of

violence.

Do not let the downtrodden be put to shame; *

let the poor and needy praise your name.

Rise up, O God, plead your cause; *

remember how the impious scoff at you all day long.

Do not forget the clamor of your foes, *

the uproar of your adversaries that goes up continually.

Glory to the Father, and to the Son,
and to the Holy Spirit. *
As it was in the beginning, is now,
and will be for ever. Amen.

Awaken my soul, awaken to Light, *
Send the darkness off in flight.

II. The Lessons *(Be seated)*

Old Testament Lesson

A reading from the book of Isaiah (50:4-10)

The Lord GOD has given me the tongue of a teacher, that I may know how to sustain the weary with a word. Morning by morning he wakens—wakens my ear to listen as those who are taught. The Lord GOD has opened my ear, and I was not rebellious, I did not turn backwards. I gave my back to those who struck me, and my cheeks to those who pulled out the beard; I did not hide my face from insult and spitting.

The Lord GOD helps me; therefore I have not been disgraced; therefore I have set my face like flint, and I know that I shall not be put to shame; he who vindicates me is near. Who will contend with me? Let us stand up together. Who are my adversaries? Let them confront me. It is the Lord GOD who helps me; who will declare me guilty? All of them will wear out like a garment; the moth will eat them up. Who among you fears the LORD and obeys the voice of his servant, who walks in darkness and has no light, yet trusts in the name of the LORD and relies upon his God?

The word of the Lord.

Silence for reflection.

Canticle

Awaken my soul, awaken this hour,
And sing for the life He gave;
He came to teach and heal in power
And point the way to save.

His love was great, so great indeed!
He came to gather the lost;
He wanted our hearts, to plant a seed,
Regardless of the cost.

But mankind was blind, they would not wait,
They could not see His love;
Because of their fear, they grew in hate,
Ignoring the God from above.

They mocked Him, and beat Him, and spat in His face,
And led Him to the cross;
They raised Him up in that awful place,
What seemed to be a loss.

But death had no strength, no power to hold,
Not able to bind Him, it's true;
Our Christ would rise once more we are told;
Forgive them, they know not what they do.

By His birth He entwined us, brought us together,
Both God and human bone;
By His death and His rising, saving us forever,
From the thought that we were alone.

So awaken my soul, awaken this hour,
And sing for the life He gave;
Live from my heart, the source of His power,
That came from an empty grave!

Br. Daniel-Joseph, CG 2012

Reading of the Gospel *(All stand)*

The Holy Gospel of Our Lord Jesus Christ according to
Matthew:

Then Jesus said to the crowds and to his disciples, "The
scribes and the Pharisees sit on Moses' seat; therefore, do
whatever they teach you and follow it; but do not do as they
do, for they do not practice what they teach. They tie up
heavy burdens, hard to bear, and lay them on the shoulders
of others; but they themselves are unwilling to lift a finger
to move them. They do all their deeds to be seen by others;
for they make their phylacteries broad and their fringes
long. They love to have the place of honor at banquets and
the best seats in the synagogues, and to be greeted with
respect in the market-places, and to have people call them
rabbi. But you are not to be called rabbi, for you have one
teacher, and you are all students."

The Gospel of the Lord.
Praise be to You, O Christ.

Be seated. Silence for reflection, homily or reading.

[The systems of this world, created by people, often clash
with the systems of God. As dispersed monastics, we live
in both worlds. How do you reconcile the two?]

Benedictus

Blessed are you O Lord our God*
You have come to your people and set them free.
You have raised up for us a mighty Savior*
Born of the house of your servant David.
Through your holy prophets you promised of old*
That you would save us from our enemies,
From the hands of all who hate us.
You promised to show mercy to our forbears*
And to remember your holy covenant.
This was the oath you swore to our father Abraham*
To set us free from the hands of our enemies,
Free to worship you without fear*
Holy and righteous in your sight all the days of our life.
And you, child, shall be called the prophet of the Most High*
For you will go before the Lord to prepare the way,
To give God's people knowledge of salvation*
Through the forgiveness of their sins.
In the tender compassion of our God*
The dawn from on high shall break upon us.
To shine on those who dwell in darkness and the shadow of death*
And to guide our feet into the way of peace.

Glory to the Father, and to the Son,
and to the Holy Spirit. *
**As it was in the beginning, is now,
and will be for ever. Amen.**

III. The Prayers

The Lord be with you all.
And also with you.

The Lord's Prayer *(Stand facing altar)*

Our Father in heaven, hallowed be your name,
   Your kingdom come, your will be done,
   On earth as it is in heaven.
Give us today our daily bread. Forgive us, as we forgive others.
   Save us from the time of trial,
 and deliver us from evil.
For the kingdom, the power, and the glory are yours
   Now and forever. Amen

Additional Prayers may be added here.

Collect

Be our Light in the darkness, O Lord, and in your great mercy defend us from all perils and dangers of this life through the love of your Son Jesus Christ, who lives and reigns with you and the Holy Spirit, one God, now and forever. **Amen.**

The grace of Our Lord Jesus Christ, and the love of God, and the companionship of the Holy Spirit, be in us and those absent from us.   **Amen.**

Let us bless the Lord.   **Thanks be to God.**

EVENING PRAYER

I. Invitatory

The officiant opens with this sentence: (All stand)

God has caused Light to shine in our hearts giving us knowledge of his love for us.

O God, make speed to save us. *
O Lord, make haste to help us.

Glory to the Father, and to the Son,
and to the Holy Spirit. *
As it was in the beginning, is now,
and will be for ever. Amen.

Phos Hilaron

O gracious Light, pure brightness of the ever-living Father in heaven, *
O Jesus Christ, holy and blessed!

Now as we have come to the setting of the sun, and our eyes behold the vesper light, *
We sing your praises, O God: Father, Son and Holy Spirit.

You are worthy at all times to be praised by happy voices, O Son of God, O Giver of life, *
And to be glorified through all the worlds.

Psalm

Blessed Jesus at your Word, *
Guide us to Thy perfect light.

Psalm 119 (125-135)

Your decrees are wonderful; *
  therefore my soul keeps them.
The unfolding of your words gives light; *
  it imparts understanding to the simple.
With open mouth I pant, *
  because I long for your commandments.
Turn to me and be gracious to me, *
  as is your custom towards those who love your name.
Keep my steps steady according to your promise, *
  and never let iniquity have dominion over me.
Redeem me from human oppression, *
  that I may keep your precepts.
Make your face shine upon your servant, *
  and teach me your statutes.
My eyes shed streams of tears *
  because your word is not kept.

Glory to the Father, and to the Son,
and to the Holy Spirit. *
**As it was in the beginning, is now,
and will be for ever. Amen.**

Blessed Jesus at your Word, *
Guide us to Thy perfect Light.

II. The Lessons *(Be seated)*

Old Testament Lesson

A reading from the Book of Wisdom (2:12-20)

Let us lay traps for this upright man, since he annoys us and opposes our way of life. he reproaches us for our sins against the Law, and accuses us of sins against our upbringing. He claims to have knowledge of God, and calls himself a child of the Lord. We see him as a reproof to our way of thinking, the very sight of him weighs our spirits down; for his kind of life is not like other people's, and his ways are quite different. In his opinion we are counterfeit; he avoids our ways as he would filth; he proclaims the final end of the upright as blessed and boasts of having God for his father. Let us see if what he says is true, and test him to see what sort of end he will have. For if the upright man is God's son, God will help him and rescue him from the clutches of his enemies. Let us test him with cruelty and torture, and thus explore this gentleness of his and put his patience to the test. Let us condemn him to a shameful death since God will rescue him - or so he claims.

The word of the Lord.

Silence for reflection.

Canticle

Arise, shine, for your Light has come,
And the glory of the Lord has dawned on you.
For behold, darkness covers the land;
Deep gloom enshrouds the peoples.

But over you the Lord will rise,
And his glory will appear upon you.
Nations will stream to your Light,
And kings to the brightness of your dawning.

Your gates will always be open;
By day or night they will never be shut.
They will call you, the City of the Lord,
The Zion of the Holy One of Israel.

Reading of the Gospel *(All stand)*

The Holy Gospel of Our Lord Jesus Christ according to Matthew:

When Jesus had finished saying all these things, he said to his disciples, "You know that after two days the Passover is coming, and the Son of Man will be handed over to be crucified." Then the chief priests and the elders of the people gathered in the palace of the high priest, who was called Caiaphas, and they conspired to arrest Jesus by stealth and kill him. But they said, "Not during the festival, or there may be a riot among the people." Then one of the twelve, who was called Judas Iscariot, went to the chief priests and said, "What will you give me if I betray him to you?" They paid him thirty pieces of silver. And from that moment Judas began to look for an opportunity to betray Jesus.

The Gospel of the Lord.
Praise be to You, O Christ.

Be seated. Silence for reflection, homily or reading.

[Living a spiritual life can be threatening to others, since it threatens the things that their dysfunctional ego thrives on. Even your own false self will rebel at times. How do you deal with this?]

Magnificat

My soul proclaims the greatness of the Lord*
    My spirit rejoices in God my Savior.
You have looked with favor on your humble servant*
    And all generations will call me blessed.
You, O God, have done great things for me*
    And holy is your name.
You have mercy on those who love you*
    From generation to generation.
You have shown the strength of your arm*
    And have scattered the proud in their conceit.
You have cast down the mighty from their thrones*
    And have lifted up the lowly,
You have filled the hungry with good things*
    And the rich you have sent away empty.
You have come to the help of your people*
    For you remembered your promise of mercy.
The promise you made to our forbears*
    To Abraham and his children forever.

Lord, O Blessed Love.
Christ, O Blessed Light.
Lord, O Blessed Love.

III. The Prayers

The Lord be with you.
And also with you.

The Lord's Prayer   *(Stand facing altar)*

Our Father in heaven, hallowed be your name,
    Your kingdom come, your will be done,
    On earth as it is in heaven.
Give us today our daily bread. Forgive us, as we forgive others.
        Save us from the time of trial,
    and deliver us from evil.
For the kingdom, the power, and the glory are yours
    Now and forever. Amen

Additional Prayers may be added here.

Collect

Gracious and merciful God, for our sake your Son became incarnate to teach, love and heal us; Give us grace to choose him as master and king, who because of mankind's failure to recognize him, was mocked with thorns and died on a cross; Grant us your Light through Jesus Christ, who lives and reigns with You and the Holy Spirit, One God, now and forever. **Amen.**

May the Lord bless us, keep us from darkness, and lead us to eternal life.   **Amen.**

Let us bless the Lord.   **Thanks be to God.**

Maundy Thursday

MORNING PRAYER

I. Invitatory

The officiant opens with this sentence: (All stand)

We are to glory in the cross of our Lord Jesus Christ, through which the love of God has been proven.

Holy and ever living God, *
By your love we are redeemed.

O Lord, Open our lips. *
And our mouth shall proclaim Your praise.

Glory to the Father, and to the Son, and to the Holy Spirit. *
As it was in the beginning, is now, and will be for ever. Amen.

Psalm

Though darkness surrounds me all, *
With you I will never fall.

Psalm 23

The LORD is my shepherd, I shall not want. *
   He makes me lie down in green pastures;
He leads me beside still waters; *
   he restores my soul.
He leads me in right paths *
   for his name's sake.
Even though I walk through the darkest valley, *
   I fear no evil for you are with me;
Your rod and your staff— *
   they comfort me.
You prepare a table before me *
   in the presence of my enemies;
You anoint my head with oil; *
   my cup overflows.
Surely goodness and mercy shall follow me *
   all the days of my life,
and I shall dwell in the house of the LORD *
   my whole life long.

Glory to the Father, and to the Son,
and to the Holy Spirit. *
**As it was in the beginning, is now,
and will be for ever. Amen.**

Though darkness surrounds me all, *
With you I will never fall.

II. The Lessons

First Reading of the Gospel *(All stand)*

The Holy Gospel of Our Lord Jesus Christ:

When it was evening, Jesus took his place with the twelve; he was troubled in spirit, and while they were eating, he said, "Truly I tell you, one of you will betray me, one who is eating with me." The disciples looked at one another, uncertain of whom he was speaking. One of his disciples—the one whom Jesus loved—was reclining next to him; Simon Peter therefore motioned to him to ask Jesus of whom he was speaking. And they became greatly distressed and began to say to him one after another, "Surely not I, Lord?" He answered, "It is one of the twelve, one who has dipped his hand into the bowl with me will betray me." So when he had dipped the piece of bread, he gave it to Judas son of Simon Iscariot. Judas, who betrayed him, said, "Surely not I, Rabbi?" He replied, "You have said so."

The Gospel of the Lord.
Praise be to You, O Christ.

Be seated. Silence for reflection, homily or reading.

[Judas' betrayal of Jesus was the tipping point that finally led to the murder of Jesus. It was predicted long ago that the collective darkness of mankind would lead to the death of Christ. But God, in His power, would turn even this horrible event into something good. Whatever bad happens to us in life, God can bring some good from it.]

Canticle

When I survey the wondrous cross
Where the young Prince of Glory died,
My richest gain I count as loss,
And pour contempt on my pride.

Forbid it Lord, that I should boast,
Save in the cross of Christ,
All the vain things that charm me most,
I sacrifice them all to love.

Were the whole realm of nature mine,
That were an offering far too small;
Love so amazing, so divine,
Demands my soul, my life, my all.

Isaac Watts (1674-1748)

Second Reading of the Gospel *(All stand)*

The Holy Gospel of Our Lord Jesus Christ:

After Judas received the piece of bread, Satan entered into him. Jesus said to him, "Do quickly what you are going to do." Now no one at the table knew why he said this to him. Some thought that, because Judas had the common purse, Jesus was telling him, "Buy what we need for the festival"; or, that he should give something to the poor. So, after receiving the piece of bread, Judas immediately went out. And it was night. "The Son of Man does as it is written of him, but woe to that one by whom the Son of Man is betrayed! It would have been better for that one not to have been born."

The Gospel of the Lord.
Praise be to You, O Christ.

Be seated. Silence for reflection, homily or reading.

[One of the worst hurts is to be betrayed by a close friend. We expect some trouble from our enemies, but not our friends. The phrase 'Satan entered into him' is one way of describing the state of mind when the false self has totally taken control of our thoughts, words, and deeds. It is at this point that there is no gap between the soul and the dysfunctional ego. The two are one. How can we prevent this from happening in ourselves? In others?]

Benedictus

Blessed are you O Lord our God*
You have come to your people and set them free.
You have raised up for us a mighty Savior*
Born of the house of your servant David.
Through your holy prophets you promised of old*
That you would save us from our enemies,
From the hands of all who hate us.
You promised to show mercy to our forbears*
And to remember your holy covenant.
This was the oath you swore to our father Abraham*
To set us free from the hands of our enemies,
Free to worship you without fear*
Holy and righteous in your sight all the days of our life.
And you, child, shall be called the prophet of the Most High*
For you will go before the Lord to prepare the way,
To give God's people knowledge of salvation*
Through the forgiveness of their sins.
In the tender compassion of our God*
The dawn from on high shall break upon us.
To shine on those who dwell in darkness and the shadow of death*
And to guide our feet into the way of peace.

Glory to the Father, and to the Son,
and to the Holy Spirit. *
**As it was in the beginning, is now,
and will be for ever. Amen.**

III. The Prayers

The Lord be with you all. *
And also with you.

The Lord's Prayer   *(Stand facing altar)*

Our Father in heaven, hallowed be your name,
    Your kingdom come, your will be done,
    On earth as it is in heaven.
Give us today our daily bread. Forgive us, as we forgive others.
    Save us from the time of trial,
    and deliver us from evil.
For the kingdom, the power, and the glory are yours
    Now and forever. Amen

Additional Prayers may be added here.

Collect

Gracious God, we praise you for this sacrament, the gift of your Son to the Church. As we share this supper together, may we know the strength of his love for us, even when he was led to the cross. Help us to enter into the fullness of this love through Jesus Christ our Lord, who lives and reigns with you and the Holy Spirit, one God, for ever and ever. **Amen.**

The grace of Our Lord Jesus Christ, and the love of God, and the companionship of the Holy Spirit, be in us and those absent from us.   **Amen.**

Let us bless the Lord.   **Thanks be to God.**

EVENING PRAYER

I. Invitatory

The officiant opens with this sentence: (All stand)

O God, make speed to save us.
O Lord, make haste to help us.

Glory to the Father, and to the Son,
and to the Holy Spirit. *
**As it was in the beginning, is now,
and will be for ever. Amen.**

Phos Hilaron

O gracious Light, pure brightness of the ever-living Father
in heaven, *
O Jesus Christ, holy and blessed!

Now as we have come to the setting of the sun, and our eyes
behold the vesper light, *
**We sing your praises, O God: Father, Son and Holy
Spirit.**

You are worthy at all times to be praised by happy voices,
O Son of God, O Giver of life, *
And to be glorified through all the worlds.

Psalm

Even my bosom friend in whom I trusted, *
He ate my bread and has lifted the heel against me.
(Ps.41:9)

Psalm 55: 12-14, 20-21

Were it an enemy who harmed me, *
that I could bear;
If an opponent pitted himself against me, *
    I could turn away from him.
But you, a person of my circle, *
    a comrade and dear friend,
to whom I was bound by close friendship *
    in the house of God!
They attack those at peace with them, *
    going back on their oaths;
though their mouth is smoother than butter, *
    enmity is in their hearts;
their words more soothing than oil, *
    yet sharpened like swords.

Glory to the Father, and to the Son,
and to the Holy Spirit. *
**As it was in the beginning, is now,
and will be forever. Amen.**

Even my bosom friend in whom I trusted, *
He ate my bread and has lifted the heel against me.

II. The Lessons *(Be seated)*

First Reading of the Gospel *(All stand)*

The Holy Gospel of Our Lord Jesus Christ:

So they went and found everything as he had told them; and they prepared the Passover meal. When the hour came, he took his place at the table, and the apostles with him. He said to them, "I have eagerly desired to eat this Passover with you before I suffer; take this and divide it among yourselves; for I tell you that from now on I will not drink of the fruit of the vine until the kingdom of God comes." While they were eating, Jesus took a loaf of bread, and after blessing it he broke it, and gave it to the disciples, saying, "Take, eat; this is my body, which is given for you. Do this in remembrance of me." Then he took the cup, and after giving thanks he gave it to them, saying, "Drink from it, all of you; for this is my blood of the new covenant, which is poured out for many." When they had sung the hymn, they went out to the Mount of Olives.

The Gospel of the Lord.
Praise be to You, O Christ.

Be seated. Silence for reflection, homily or reading.

[Jesus' act of sharing the meal represents the love of **God**; the bread represents the Body of **Christ** - that which St. Paul described as including each and every one of us; the wine represents the life blood and power of the **Holy Spirit** - that which fuels our desire and understanding to go out and spread the love of God to others, using the unique gifts and talents God has given to each of us.]

59

Canticle

My Shepherd will supply my need,
Jesus is his name;
In pastures fresh he gives me feed,
Beside the living stream.
He brings my wandering spirit back
When I forsake his ways,
And leads me, for his mercy's sake,
In paths of truth and grace.

When I walk through the valley of death,
Thy presence does near me stay;
One word of thy supporting breath
Drives all my fears away.
Thy hand in sight of all my foes,
Does still my table spread;
My cup with blessings flows,
Thy oil anoints my head.

The sure provisions of my God
Attend me all my days;
O may thy house be my abode,
And all my work be praise.
There would I find a settled rest,
While others go and come;
No more a stranger or a guest,
But like a child at home.

Isaac Watts (1674-1748), based on Psalm 23

Second Reading of the Gospel *(All stand)*

The Holy Gospel of Our Lord Jesus Christ:

Then Jesus went with them to a place called Gethsemane; and he said to his disciples, "Sit here while I go over there and pray." He took with him Peter and the two sons of Zebedee, and began to be grieved and agitated. Then he said to them, "I am deeply grieved, even to death; remain here, and stay awake with me." And going a little farther, he threw himself on the ground and prayed, "My Father, if it is possible, let this cup pass from me; yet not what I want but what you want." Then he came to the disciples and found them sleeping; and he said to Peter, "So, could you not stay awake with me one hour? Stay awake and pray that you may not come into the time of trial; the spirit indeed is willing, but the flesh is weak." Again he went away for the second time and prayed, "My Father, if this cannot pass unless I drink it, your will be done." Again he came and found them sleeping, for their eyes were heavy. So leaving them again, he went away and prayed for the third time, saying the same words. Then he came to the disciples and said to them, "Are you still sleeping and taking your rest? See, the hour is at hand, and the Son of Man is betrayed into the hands of sinners. Get up, let us be going. See, my betrayer is at hand."

The Gospel of the Lord.
Praise be to You, O Christ.

Be seated. Silence for reflection, homily or reading.

[It is not always easy to do the will of God. Sometimes it appears that the short-term costs are too high. But let us look to the long-term result - the ultimate fulfillment of God's plan for us and others.]

Magnificat

My soul proclaims the greatness of the Lord*
    My spirit rejoices in God my Savior.
You have looked with favor on your humble servant*
    And all generations will call me blessed.
You, O God, have done great things for me*
    And holy is your name.
You have mercy on those who love you*
    From generation to generation.
You have shown the strength of your arm*
    And have scattered the proud in their conceit.
You have cast down the mighty from their thrones*
    And have lifted up the lowly,
You have filled the hungry with good things*
    And the rich you have sent away empty.
You have come to the help of your people*
    For you remembered your promise of mercy.
The promise you made to our forbears*
    To Abraham and his children forever.

Lord, O Blessed Love.
Christ, O Blessed Light.
Lord, O Blessed Love.

III. The Prayers

The Lord be with you.
And also with you.

The Lord's Prayer   *(Stand facing altar)*

Our Father in heaven, hallowed be your name,
    Your kingdom come, your will be done,
    On earth as it is in heaven.
Give us today our daily bread. Forgive us, as we forgive
others.
        Save us from the time of trial,
    and deliver us from evil.
For the kingdom, the power, and the glory are yours
    Now and forever. Amen

Additional Prayers may be added here.

Collect

Almighty Father, whose dear Son, on the night before he
suffered, instituted the Sacrament of the Eucharist;
Mercifully grant that we may receive it thankfully in
remembrance of Jesus Christ, our Lord, who in these holy
mysteries gives us a pledge of eternal life; and who now
lives and reigns with You and the Holy Spirit, One God,
now and forever. **Amen.**

May the Lord bless us, keep us from evil, and lead us to
eternal life.   **Amen.**

Let us bless the Lord.   **Thanks be to God.**

Good Friday
The Crucifixion

Invitatory

The officiant opens with this sentence: (All stand)

The collective darkness of mankind slew our Lord,
but this did not diminish his love for us!

We follow the path of the cross today,
To know what our Lord did suffer;
May he open our hearts in a new way,
To learn the things he did offer.
To the world his love he can now offer.

Glory to the Father, and to the Son,
and to the Holy Spirit. *
As it was in the beginning, is now,
and will be for ever. Amen.

Preparatory Prayer

O Most Merciful Jesus, with an open and contrite heart, I
ask for your Divine Presence on this journey of the Cross.
Through your life you provided us with the wisdom to live
an upright and just life; through your death you
demonstrated what the depth of mankind's darkness could
do without you; and through your resurrection you proved
that nothing can diminish your love for us, not even death
itself. I again ask for your continued guidance and support
that I may yet begin again. Amen.

The Stations

Station 1. Jesus is condemned to death.
(6:30 am)

We adore you, O Christ, and bless you. *
Through your love you have redeemed the world.

A Reading from the Gospel of our Lord Jesus Christ:

When morning came, all the chief priests and the elders of
the people conferred together against Jesus in order to bring
about his death. They bound him, and handed him over to
Pilate the governor. The governor asked him, "Are you the
King of the Jews?" Jesus said, "You say so." Then Pilate
said to him, "Do you not hear how many accusations they
make against you?" But he gave him no answer, not even to
a single charge, so that the governor was greatly amazed.

Now at the festival the governor was accustomed to
release a prisoner for the crowd, anyone whom they wanted.
At that time they had a notorious prisoner, called Barabbas.
So after they had gathered, Pilate said to them, "Whom do
you want me to release for you, Barabbas or Jesus who is
called the Messiah?" For he realized that it was out of
jealousy that they had handed him over. While he was
sitting on the judgment seat, his wife sent word to him,
"Have nothing to do with that innocent man, for today I
have suffered a great deal because of a dream about him."

Now the chief priests and the elders persuaded the
crowds to ask for Barabbas and to have Jesus killed. The
governor again said to them, "Which of the two do you
want me to release for you?" And they said, "Barabbas!"
Pilate said to them, "Then what should I do with Jesus who
is called the Messiah?"

All of them said, "Let him be crucified!" Then he asked, "Why, what evil has he done?"

But they shouted all the more, "Let him be crucified!" So when Pilate saw that he could do nothing, but rather that a riot was beginning, he took some water and washed his hands before the crowd, saying, "I am innocent of this man's blood; see to it yourselves." Then the people as a whole answered, "His blood be on us and on our children!" So he released Barabbas for them; and after flogging Jesus, he handed him over to be crucified.

The Gospel of the Lord.

Praise be to You, O Christ.

Silence for reflection.

[Jesus was condemned to death following false accusations. People may hold false perceptions of others or themselves because of the illusions and prejudices covering their soul. This can lead to harm and damage to others or to ourselves. Are you always affirming of others, or have you sometimes been critical? Are there any injustices done to you that still have to be healed?]

Lord, we see what can happen when we hold false ideas about others or ourselves in our minds. Grant that we hold only the image of you when we look upon others or ourselves before we allow any thought in our mind, or take any action. **Amen**.

Station 2. Jesus carries his cross.
(6:45 am)

We adore you, O Christ, and bless you. *
Through your love you have redeemed the world.

A Reading from the Gospel of our Lord Jesus Christ according to John:

So they took Jesus; and carrying the cross by himself, he went out to what is called The Place of the Skull, which in Hebrew is called Golgotha.

The Gospel of the Lord.

Praise be to You, O Christ.

Silence for reflection.

[Jesus was forced to carry the cross that would be used to crucify him. Sometimes we have to carry a burden that doesn't necessarily belong to us. Sometimes we agree to carry another's burden. If we think about how we are all interconnected, all part of God's one family, then, as St. Paul says, when one person is suffering, we all are suffering. If one person has to carry a cross, then a part of us has to carry that cross, too. This is what Jesus was demonstrating for us. We must work together.]

Lord, help me remain open to the needs of others. Not that I can solve everyone's problems, but I can be with them in thought, word and prayer. And where I have the power to take action, show me the way. **Amen.**

Station 3. Jesus falls the first time.
(7:00 am)

We adore you, O Christ, and bless you. *
Through your love you have redeemed the world.

Jesus soon stumbled under the weight and size of the cross.

Praise be to You, O Christ.

Silence for reflection.

[Our spiritual journey is often punctuated with stumbles and falls. Sometimes the falls teach us, sometimes they make us stronger, and sometimes they just hurt. When this happens, we find the strength through Christ to get up and continue on. Who can help you with this?]

Lord, be with me and give me strength as I walk the spiritual journey. **Amen.**

Station 4. Jesus meets his mother.
(7:15 am)

We adore you, O Christ, and bless you. *
Through your love you have redeemed the world.

Jesus meets his mother while carrying the cross to Golgotha.

Hail Mary, full of grace, the Lord is with you. Blessed are you among women and blessed is the fruit of your womb, Jesus. Holy Mary, mother of God, pray for us, His children, now and at the hour of our death. **Amen.**

Praise be to You, O Christ.

Silence for reflection.

[The ties of family carry special bonds, but can also be the source of deeper hurt. There are hurts in life we cannot spare our loved ones. Who has been special to you in your life? Have you hurt anyone that needs amends?]

Lord, help me to know the members of my family more deeply, that we may understand each other more truly. **Amen.**

Station 5. Simon helps Jesus.
(7:30 am)

We adore you, O Christ, and bless you. *
Through your love you have redeemed the world.

A Reading from the Gospel of our Lord Jesus Christ:

On their way out to Golgotha, they seized a man from
Cyrene who was coming in from the country, called Simon,
father of Alexander and Rufus, and made him shoulder the
cross and carry it behind Jesus for a while.

The Gospel of the Lord.

Praise be to You, O Christ.

Silence for reflection.

[Sometimes we are called upon to help others, and
sometimes we do it willingly. But either way, we do it with
the help of the Lord. What can help you to respond
generously?]

Lord, help me to see the needs of others and respond
appropriately. Help me to serve with my heart when called
upon. **Amen.**

Station 6. Veronica wipes the face of Jesus.
(7:45 am)

We adore you, O Christ, and bless you. *
Through your love you have redeemed the world.

A woman came out of the crowd to get close to Jesus. Her name was Veronica. She takes her veil and begins to wipe the blood and sweat from Jesus' face. Jesus' holy countenance is imprinted on this act through the veil.

Praise be to You, O Christ.

Silence for reflection.

[Tradition holds that an image of Jesus appeared on the veil of Veronica. This should not be too unusual, since all good works carry the spirit and image of Christ in our hearts, wherever and whenever performed. Who do you look to for comfort? Do you know of someone in need of comforting?]

Lord, help me to hold the image of Christ in my heart, and help me to see it in the hearts of others. **Amen.**

Station 7. Jesus falls the second time.
(8:00 am)

We adore you, O Christ, and bless you. *
Through your love you have redeemed the world.

Jesus, once again carrying the cross, stumbles again under its weight. His strength is diminishing, and the crowds jeers and taunts are growing. The soldiers continue pushing and striking him, making him rise and continue on.

Praise be to You, O Christ.

Silence for reflection.

[Our journey through life is rarely without troubles and trials. Just because we claim the love of God in our hearts does not mean that the journey will be smooth. It does mean, however, that God will be with us along the way. In what ways do you keep 'tripping up'? Who can help you with this?]

Lord, be my strength as I walk the path. **Amen.**

Station 8. Jesus meets the women of Jerusalem.
(8:15 am)

We adore you, O Christ, and bless you. *
Through your love you have redeemed the world.

A Reading from the Gospel of our Lord Jesus Christ:

Large numbers of people followed him, including the
women of Jerusalem, who mourned and lamented for him.
But Jesus turned to them and said, "Daughters of Jerusalem,
do not weep for me; weep rather for yourselves and for your
children. The days are surely coming when people will say,
'Blessed are those who are barren, the wombs that have
never borne children, the breasts that have never suckled!'
Then they will begin to say to the mountains, 'Fall on us!'
and to the hills, 'Cover us!' For if this is what is done to
green wood, what will be done when the wood is dry?"

The Gospel of the Lord.

Praise be to You, O Christ.

Silence for reflection.

[Sometimes our own sufferings can be diminished when we
help others with their sufferings. We can make choices.
Who do you know that is in need of help?]

Lord, give us a joyful attitude, and help us to help others.
Amen.

Station 9. Jesus falls a third time.
(8:30 am)

We adore you, O Christ, and bless you. *
Through your love you have redeemed the world.

Arriving exhausted at the foot of Calvary, Jesus falls yet
again. Although physically exhausted, his resolve to
complete his mission carries him forward even though the
worst still awaits him.

Praise be to You, O Christ.

Silence for reflection.

[Continuing to stumble in what we try to do can cause us to
give up trying. But this is where faith and the support of
Christ enter in. Do you sometimes feel like giving up?
What keeps you going?]

Lord, lift us up one time more than when we fall. **Amen.**

Station 10. Jesus is stripped of his garments.
(8:45 am)

We adore you, O Christ, and bless you. *
Through your love you have redeemed the world.

A Reading from the Gospel of our Lord Jesus Christ:

The soldiers took Jesus's clothing and divided it into four shares, one for each soldier. One of his garments was seamless, woven in one piece from neck to hem. So the soldiers said to one another, "Instead of tearing it, let's throw dice to decide who is to have it." In this way the words of scripture were fulfilled: "They divide my garments among them and cast lots for my clothes."

The Gospel of the Lord.

Praise be to You, O Christ.

Silence for reflection.

[Many of us carry the wounds of abuses and humiliations caused by others. Christ knows what this is like. What do you think he wants to tell you about this?]

Lord, show us that regardless of our life's experiences, you hold us in the dignity of love. **Amen.**

Station 11. Jesus is nailed to the cross.
(9:00 am)

We adore you, O Christ, and bless you. *
Through your love you have redeemed the world.

A Reading from the Gospel of our Lord Jesus Christ:

Then they crucified Jesus on the cross at the place of the skull, Golgotha along with two others, one on his right, the other on his left. Jesus said, "Father, forgive them; they do not know what they are doing."

The Gospel of the Lord.

Praise be to You, O Christ.

Silence for reflection.

[Jesus was trapped. Do you sometimes feel trapped by life; that there is no way out of problems? Have these experiences ever provided you with a new beginning that you didn't realize before?]

Lord, give us a trusting heart in times of peril and struggle.
Amen.

NOON to 3:00pm - GREATER SILENCE
It was now about noon, and a darkness came over the whole land until about 3pm.

Station 12. Jesus dies on the cross.
(3:00 pm)

We adore you, O Christ, and bless you. *
Through your love you have redeemed the world.

A Reading from the Gospel of our Lord Jesus Christ:

In the ninth hour (about 3pm), Jesus cited Psalm 22 by crying out, "My God, my God, why have you forsaken me?" When some of those who stood there heard this, they said, "The man is calling on Elijah." One of them quickly ran to get a sponge which he filled with vinegar and, putting it on a reed, gave it to him to drink. But the rest of the people said, "Wait! See if Elijah will come to save him." But Jesus cried out in a loud voice saying, "Father, it is finished. Into your hands I commit my spirit." With these words he bowed his head and breathed his last. Suddenly the veil of the Sanctuary was torn in two from top to bottom, the earth shook, and rocks were split. A centurion saw all that was taking place and said, "In truth this man was the Son of God."

The Gospel of the Lord. **Praise be to You, O Christ.**

Silence for reflection.

[Full contact comes with God when we "commit our spirit" to him. It is at this point that we are all his, and we are one with him.]

Lord, help us to invite you into our lives, completely.
Amen.

Station 13. The body of Jesus is taken down.
(4:00 pm)

We adore you, O Christ, and bless you. *
Through your love you have redeemed the world.

A Reading from the Gospel of our Lord Jesus Christ:

After this, Joseph of Arimathaea, who was a follower of
Jesus - though a secret one because he was afraid of the
Jews - asked Pilate to let him remove the body of Jesus.
Pilate gave permission, so he came and took it away.

The Gospel of the Lord.

Praise be to You, O Christ.

Silence for reflection.

[Jesus waited to be taken down from the cross and to be laid
to rest. We, too, often have to wait before we are helped.
Grocery check-out lines, traffic lights, the check coming in
the mail, or pain relief. When we help others shorten their
wait, we help Jesus down from the cross.]

Lord, help me to accept the things I cannot change, and to
change the things I can; and grant me the wisdom to know
the difference. **Amen.**

Station 14. Jesus is laid in the tomb.
(5:00 pm)

We adore you, O Christ, and bless you. *
Through your love you have redeemed the world.

A Reading from the Gospel of our Lord Jesus Christ:

Joseph of Arimathaea took the body of Jesus, wrapped it in
a clean shroud, and put it in his own tomb which he had
hewn out of the rock, and which never held a body.
Nicodemus came as well - the same one who had first come
to Jesus at night-time - and he brought a mixture of myrrh
and aloes, weighing about a hundred pounds. They took the
body of Jesus and bound it in linen cloths with the spices,
following the Jewish burial custom. Then they rolled a
large stone across the entrance of the tomb and went away.
Mary of Magdala and the other Mary were there, sitting
opposite the sepulcher.

The Gospel of the Lord. **Praise be to You, O Christ.**

III. Concluding Prayer

Merciful God, creator of all peoples and lover of every soul;
have compassion on all who do not know you, let your
Gospel be heard in every heart through your Spirit, warm
the hearts of those who oppose it, and bring home to your
pasture any who have gone astray; through Jesus Christ our
Lord, who lives and reigns with you and the Holy Spirit,
one God, now and forever. **Amen.**

Holy Saturday

MORNING PRAYER

I. Invitatory

The officiant opens with this sentence: (All stand)

Even Christ's death at the hands of mankind did not alter God's love for us, but proved it; and now we shall be saved by his life. (Romans 5:10)

He was crucified, died and was buried; *
He descended to the dead.

O Lord, Open our lips. *
And our mouth shall proclaim Your praise.

Glory to the Father, and to the Son,
and to the Holy Spirit. *
**As it was in the beginning, is now,
and will be for ever. Amen.**

Psalm *(from Psalm 96)*

The stone that the builders rejected *
Has become the chief cornerstone.

O sing to the LORD a new song; *
 sing to the LORD, all the earth.
Sing to the LORD, bless his name; *
 tell of his salvation from day to day.
Declare his glory among the nations, *
 his marvelous works among all the peoples.
For great is the LORD, and greatly to be praised; *
 he is to be revered above all gods.
For all the gods of the peoples are idols, *
 but the LORD made the heavens.
Honor and majesty are before him; *
 strength and beauty are in his sanctuary.
Ascribe to the LORD the glory due his name; *
 bring an offering, and come into his courts.
Say among the nations, 'The LORD is king! *
 The world is firmly established; it shall never be moved.
He will judge the peoples with equity.' *
 Let the heavens be glad, and let the earth rejoice;
Let the sea roar, and all that fills it; *
 Let the field exult, and everything in it.
He will judge the world with righteousness, *
 and the peoples with his truth.

Glory to the Father, and to the Son,
and to the Holy Spirit. *
As it was in the beginning, is now,
and will be for ever. Amen.

The stone that the builders rejected *
Has become the chief cornerstone.

II. The Lessons *(Be seated)*

New Testament Lesson

A reading from the book of 1 Peter:

Christ was put to death in the flesh, but made alive in the
spirit, in which also he went and made a proclamation to the
spirits in prison, who in former times did not obey, when
God waited patiently in the days of Noah, during the
building of the ark, in which a few, that is, eight people,
were saved through water. And baptism, which this
prefigured, now saves you—not as a removal of dirt from
the body, but as an appeal to God for a good conscience,
through the resurrection of Jesus Christ, who has gone into
heaven and is at the right hand of God, with angels,
authorities, and powers made subject to him. For this is the
reason the gospel was proclaimed even to the dead, so that,
though they had been judged in the flesh as everyone is
judged, they might live in the spirit as God does.
The word of the Lord.

Silence for reflection.

Canticle

Were you there when they crucified my Lord?
Sometimes it causes me to tremble.

Were you there when they nailed him to a tree?
Sometimes it causes me to tremble.

Were you there when they pierced him in his side?
Sometimes it causes me to tremble.

Were you there when they laid him in the tomb?
Sometimes it causes me to tremble.

From an Afro-American spiritual

Reading of the Gospel *(All stand)*

The Holy Gospel of Our Lord Jesus Christ according to
Matthew (27:62-66)

The next day, that is, after the day of Preparation, the chief
priests and the Pharisees gathered before Pilate and said,
"Sir, we remember what that impostor said while he was
still alive, 'After three days I will rise again.' Therefore
command that the tomb be made secure until the third day;
otherwise his disciples may go and steal him away, and tell
the people, 'He has been raised from the dead', and the last
deception would be worse than the first." Pilate said to
them, "You have a guard of soldiers; go, make it as secure
as you can." So they went with the guard and made the
tomb secure by sealing the stone.

The Gospel of the Lord.
Praise be to You, O Christ.

Be seated. Silence for reflection, homily or reading.

[The plans and power of God cannot be stopped by anything that mankind can think, do, or say. Can you accept that he is working out your life for you in his own way?]

Benedictus

Blessed are you O Lord our God*
You have come to your people and set them free.
You have raised up for us a mighty Savior*
Born of the house of your servant David.
Through your holy prophets you promised of old*
That you would save us from our enemies,
From the hands of all who hate us.
You promised to show mercy to our forbears*
And to remember your holy covenant.
This was the oath you swore to our father Abraham*
To set us free from the hands of our enemies,
Free to worship you without fear*
Holy and righteous in your sight all the days of our life.
And you, child, shall be called the prophet of the Most High*
For you will go before the Lord to prepare the way,
To give God's people knowledge of salvation*
Through the forgiveness of their sins.
In the tender compassion of our God*
The dawn from on high shall break upon us.
To shine on those who dwell in darkness and the shadow of death*
And to guide our feet into the way of peace.

Glory to the Father, and to the Son,
and to the Holy Spirit. *
As it was in the beginning, is now,
and will be for ever. Amen.

III. The Prayers

The Lord be with you all.
And also with you.

The Lord's Prayer   *(Stand facing altar)*

Our Father in heaven, hallowed be your name,
    Your kingdom come, your will be done,
    On earth as it is in heaven.
Give us today our daily bread. Forgive us, as we forgive
others.
    Save us from the time of trial,
 and deliver us from evil.
For the kingdom, the power, and the glory are yours
    Now and forever. Amen

Additional Prayers may be added here.

Collect

O God, Creator of heaven and earth: Grant that, as the body of Your Son lay in the tomb and rested on this holy Sabbath, so may we await his return through resurrection, and rise with him to newness of life; who now lives and reigns with You and the Holy Spirit, One God, now and forever. **Amen.**

The grace of Our Lord Jesus Christ, and the love of God, and the companionship of the Holy Spirit, be in us and those absent from us.   **Amen.**

Let us bless the Lord.   **Thanks be to God.**

EVENING PRAYER

I. Invitatory

The officiant opens with this sentence: (All stand)

Since Christ created us once out of his love and mercy, why not again?

O God, make speed to save us.
O Lord, make haste to help us.

Glory to the Father, and to the Son,
and to the Holy Spirit. *
**As it was in the beginning, is now,
and will be for ever. Amen.**

Phos Hilaron

O gracious Light, pure brightness of
the ever-living Father in heaven, *
O Jesus Christ, holy and blessed!

Now as we have come to the setting of the sun, and our eyes
behold the vesper light, *
**We sing your praises, O God: Father, Son and Holy
Spirit.**

You are worthy at all times to be praised by happy voices,
O Son of God, O Giver of life, *
And to be glorified through all the worlds.

Psalm *(from Psalm 30)*

For I know that my Redeemer lives, *
In the end he will stand upon the earth.

I will extol you, O LORD, for you have drawn me up, *
    and did not let my foes rejoice over me.
O LORD my God, I cried to you for help, *
    and you have healed me.
O LORD, you brought up my soul from Sheol, *
    restored me to life from those gone down to the Pit.
Sing praises to the LORD, O you his faithful ones, *
    and give thanks to his holy name.
For his anger is but for a moment; *
    his favor is for a lifetime.
Weeping may linger for the night, *
    but joy comes with the morning.
To you, O LORD, I cried, *
    and to you I made supplication:
'What profit is there in my death, *
    if I go down to the Pit?
Will the dust praise you? *
    Will it tell of your faithfulness?
Hear, O LORD, and be gracious to me! *
    O LORD, be my helper!'
You have turned my mourning into dancing; *
    O LORD my God, I will give thanks to you forever.

Glory to the Father, and to the Son,
and to the Holy Spirit. *
**As it was in the beginning, is now,
and will be for ever. Amen.**

For I know that my Redeemer lives, *
In the end he will stand upon the earth.

II. The Lessons *(Be seated)*

New Testament Lesson

A reading from the Book of Romans *(chapter 8)*:

There is therefore now no condemnation for those who are in Christ Jesus. For the teachings of the Spirit of life in Christ Jesus has set you free from the law of sin and of death. For God has done what the law, weakened by the mind, could not do: by sending his own Son in the likeness of mankind, and to deal with sin, he condemned sin in the world, so that the just requirement of the law might be fulfilled in us, who walk not according to the mind but according to the Spirit. For those who live according to the world set their minds on the things of the world, but those who live according to the Spirit set their minds on the things of the Spirit. To set the mind on the world is death, but to set the mind on the Spirit is life and peace. For this reason the mind that is set on the world is hostile to God; it does not submit to God's law—indeed it cannot, and those who live in mankind's ways cannot please God. But you are not in the world; you are in the Spirit, since the Spirit of God dwells in you. Anyone who does not have the Spirit of Christ does not belong to him. But if Christ is in you, though the body is dead because of sin, the Spirit is life because of righteousness. If the Spirit of him who raised Jesus from the dead dwells in you, he who raised Christ from the dead will give life to your mortal bodies also through his Spirit that dwells in you.

The Word of the Lord.

Silence for reflection.

Canticle

Day by day, dear Lord,

Of Thee three things I pray:

To see Thee more clearly,

To love Thee more dearly,

To follow Thee more nearly,

Day by day.

Richard of Chichester (1197-1253)

Reading of the Gospel *(All stand)*

The Holy Gospel of Our Lord Jesus Christ according to Luke (23:55-56)

The women who had come with him from Galilee followed, and they saw the tomb and how his body was laid. Then they returned, and prepared spices and ointments. On the Sabbath they rested according to the commandment.

The Gospel of the Lord.
Praise be to You, O Christ.

Be seated. Silence for reflection, homily or reading.

[The Sabbath day is a pause in the creation of the week. Even during this time of great sadness and uncertainty, when everything seemed to be coming apart, the people around Jesus still rested and waited. They had faith and hope that Jesus' promises would be fulfilled. You can, too.]

Magnificat

My soul proclaims the greatness of the Lord*
    My spirit rejoices in God my Savior.
You have looked with favor on your humble servant*
    And all generations will call me blessed.
You, O God, have done great things for me*
    And holy is your name.
You have mercy on those who love you*
    From generation to generation.
You have shown the strength of your arm*
    And have scattered the proud in their conceit.
You have cast down the mighty from their thrones*
    And have lifted up the lowly,
You have filled the hungry with good things*
    And the rich you have sent away empty.
You have come to the help of your people*
    For you remembered your promise of mercy.
The promise you made to our forbears*
    To Abraham and his children forever.

Lord, O Blessed Love.
Christ, O Blessed Light.
Lord, O Blessed Love.

III. The Prayers

The Lord be with you.
And also with you.

The Lord's Prayer   *(Stand facing altar)*

Our Father in heaven, hallowed be your name,
　Your kingdom come, your will be done,
　On earth as it is in heaven.
Give us today our daily bread. Forgive us, as we forgive
others.
　Save us from the time of trial,
　and deliver us from evil.
For the kingdom, the power, and the glory are yours
　Now and forever. Amen

Additional Prayers may be added here.

Collect

Grant O God, that our prejudices, illusions, fears, worries
and shame all die and are buried with the death of Christ,
that through the grave and the gate of death we may pass to
our joyful resurrection to a new life, in this world and the
next, living in the Light of his love, through Jesus Christ our
Lord, who lives and reigns with you and the Holy Spirit,
one God now and forever more. **Amen.**

May the God of hope fill you with all joy and peace in
believing, so that you may abound in hope by the power of
the Holy Spirit. **Amen.**

Let us bless the Lord.   **Thanks be to God.**

About the Author

Daniel D. Schroeder completed his undergraduate studies in Classical Hebrew at the University of Wisconsin-Milwaukee. He is the founder of the Community of the Gospel, a dispersed monastic Episcopal Christian Community which has members across the United States. Daniel also has a Master of Science in adult educational psychology and an MBA in finance. He and his wife live in east central Wisconsin. Daniel can be reached at:

BeneVentura, LLC
PO Box 414
Hortonville, WI 54944

www.communityofthegospel.org

CPSIA information can be obtained
at www.ICGtesting.com
Printed in the USA
BVOW06s1507120317
478088BV00007B/36/P